Secrets of
Comfort and Joy

J. Donald Walters

Hardbound edition 2000

Copyright © 2000 by Crystal Clarity Publishers

ISBN 1-56589-131-7
1 3 5 7 9 10 8 6 4 2

Photographs: J. Donald Walters
Cover and book design by C. A. Starner Schuppe

Printed in China

14618 Tyler Foote Road,
Nevada City, CA 95959-8599

800-424-1055 ◆ 530-478-7600
www.crystalclarity.com

A seed thought is offered for every day of the month. Begin a day at the appropriate date. Repeat the saying several times: first out loud, then softly, then in a whisper, and then only mentally. With each repetition, allow the words to become absorbed ever more deeply into your subconscious.

Thus, gradually, you will acquire a complete under-standing of each day's thought. At this point, indeed, the truths set forth here will have become your own.

Keep the book open at the pertinent page throughout the day. Refer to it occasionally during moments of leisure. Relate the saying as often as possible to real situations in your life.

Then at night, before you go to bed, repeat the thought several times more. While falling asleep, carry the words into your subconscious, absorbing their positive influence into your whole being. Let it become thereby an integral part of your normal consciousness.

Love all, for by loving
we live in joy,
but by hating or resenting others
we experience only
deep inner restlessness and pain.

Day One

*U*nderstand that
true satisfaction is found
not in endless variety,
but in inner stillness.

D a y   T w o

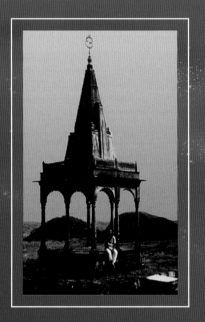

Show mercy,
when you have the power
to avenge a wrong.
Revenge merely increases
one's sense of injury.
But relief comes
from banishing
even the consciousness
that you've been wronged.

Day Three

By giving comfort
to others,
we ourselves find comfort.
By giving joy,
we ourselves find joy.
When we channel
God's love to all,
comfort and joy abide,
smilingly, in our hearts.

Day Four

Greet every trial with a smile,
and remain undaunted.
Trials are not the misfortunes
they so often seem:
They are opportunities!
Comfort comes
only after challenges
have been met and overcome.
It never comes to those
who seek to avoid them.

Day Five

Share with others
a kind smile;
a word of appreciation
or encouragement.
Joy and comfort expand
to fill any niche
you create for them.

Day Six

*D*o something *today*
to bring solace
to some grieving heart.
In this service,
try earnestly to feel
God's love.

Day Seven

*C*oncentrate
on the qualities you like
and admire in others.
You'll be reassured
of your own capacity
for self-improvement.

Day Eight

Recall times when others have given to you sincerely of themselves. Rejoice in their friendship; take comfort from it: It is your greatest earthly treasure. Sincere friendship is a living proof that love IS.

Day Nine

Seek practical ways
of helping others.
Abstract principles
must be clothed
in outer forms
if they are to become
fully real for us.

Day Ten

*P*ray for someone
who considers himself
your enemy.
Offer his enmity up to God.
Whether that prayer wins him
as a friend or not,
your heart will be comforted
in knowing that nothing
can ever rob you
of your own peace of mind.

Day Eleven

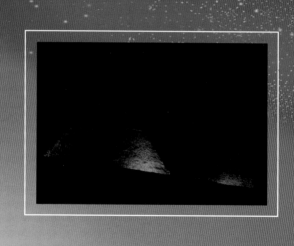

*B*e centered
in your inner self.
Let nothing and no one
disturb you.
Though you are
surrounded by change,
live in the awareness
of changelessness.

Day Twelve

*K*eep your mind fixed
on your highest priorities.
Above all,
make God's truth
your polestar.
Let the ship of your life
never veer
from its right course.

Day Thirteen

*A*ffirm joy
as your abiding reality.
Don't wait for happiness
to come to you:
It is yours already!
Joy underlies every thought,
every feeling.
With this simple recognition,
comfort will be yours always.

Day Fourteen

Remember:
Joy belongs to
the present moment!
It can be yours only *today*.
Don't wait for it to come to you
at some hoped-for time
in the future.

Day Fifteen

*U*nderstand the difference
between desire-fulfillment
and true joy.
Joy is native to the inner Self.
Fulfilled desire, however,
brings no lasting comfort.
All things change,
and are therefore unreliable.
Outside the Self,
where can security be found?

Day Sixteen

Seek not your joy
in emotions,
for their fluctuations
are unceasing.
Seek it rather in calmness.
True joy, like an ocean,
rests quietly beneath the waves
of restless feeling.

Day Seventeen

*C*omfort and joy,
like pink blossoms,
flower on the tree of life
when your conscience is clear,
and like sap is able to flow freely.
To keep the sap fluid,
irrigate your tree daily
with truthfulness, kind thoughts,
and generous deeds.

Day Eighteen

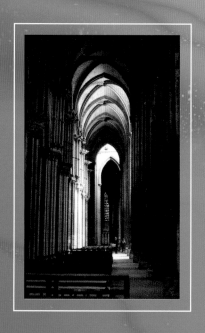

*U*nderstand that joy
is not something you can
obtain by outward effort,
or by affirmation.
It can only be
discovered in yourself.
Keep your heart open, and
your mind at rest.

Day Nineteen

*J*oy is not the fruit
of excitement,
but of deep calmness.
Calmness is the cherry tree
of inner detachment,
of which the fruit
is not indifference, but joy.

Day Twenty

When any bubble of joy
appears in your
consciousness, expand it.
Let it first fill your being,
then expand further
to include other lives:
those known to you,
and also those unknown.

Day Twenty-one

*T*hank God daily —
not so much for His gifts
as for His love.
That love has been yours
since the very dawn of time!
In thankfulness,
recognize love
as the deepest truth
of your own being.

Day Twenty-two

*L*ove is the hidden blessing
behind all of life's trials.
They are sent to test
your sensitivity to it.
Remember, without combat
the warrior's skill
cannot be developed.

Day Twenty-three

*A*ccept no failure
as destiny's final decree for you.
"The season of failure,"
it has been wisely said,
"is the best time
for planting the seeds
of success."

Day Twenty-four

*F*rom today onward,
affirm courage!
Forget past shames:
Hasn't every human being
erred at some time?
Define yourself,
and others also,
by your souls' high potential.

Day Twenty-five

*L*ook upon your family
as a gift from God.
If by familiarity
your appreciation of it
has been dulled,
look beyond,
to the Eternal Friend.
God endeavors through others
to shape us in the image
of His love.

Day Twenty-six

*Forgive those
who have deeply hurt you.
Forgiveness will develop in you
the ability to forgive yourself.
Release all
your painful memories,
like birds soaring in skies
of mental freedom.*

Day Twenty-seven

$\mathcal{B}$e aware of God's love
behind the gift of human love.
For human love
brings anguish and uncertainty,
but divine love
brings inward reassurance
and constant joy.

$\mathcal{D}$ay $\mathcal{T}$wenty-eight

Reflect:
You belong to no one,
and no one belongs to you.
In true love
there is no possessiveness.
True love is the gift
of inner freedom.

Day Twenty-nine

Comfort and joy
are the glad tidings
of God's love.
Rejoice in others' happiness.
Let your comfort and joy
expand everywhere,
to embrace all.

Day Thirty

$\mathcal{C}$omfort and joy
will be yours
when you can accept
the griefs of others,
and hold them up for comfort
to God's love.

Day Thirty-one

Selected Other Titles
by J. Donald Walters:

Art as a Hidden Message
Education for Life
Do It Now!
Expansive Marriage
Money Magnetism
The Art of Supportive Leadership
Affirmations for Self-Healing
The Path (the autobiography
of J. Donald Walters)

For information about these or other Crystal Clarity
books, tapes, or products call:
800-424-1055 or 530-478-7600
Or visit our website: *www.crystalclarity.com*